LNER Locomotives

in colour
1936–1948

Ron White and Norman Johnston

6 5 4 3 2 1

© Colourpoint Books
Newtownards 2002

Designed by Colourpoint Books,
Newtownards

Printed by Nicholson & Bass Ltd

ISBN 1 898392 27 7

Colourpoint Books
Unit D5, Ards Business Centre
Jubilee Road
NEWTOWNARDS
County Down
Northern Ireland
BT23 4YH
Tel: 028 9182 0505
Fax: 028 9182 1900
E-mail: info@colourpoint.co.uk
Web-site: www.colourpoint.co.uk

Ron White (left) is well known in railway circles as 'Mr ColourRail' and has been responsible for saving many priceless collections of colour slides for posterity.

Norman Johnston (right) is author of *Locomotives of the GNRI* and co-author of *Fermanagh's Railways*. He has been interested in the history of railway locomotives from his teenage years.

Cover photographs:

Front

A3 4-6-2 No 2582 *Sir Hugo* in the engine bay at Grantham in August 1946. This superb photograph shows the post-war LNER apple green livery off to advantage as well as capturing many of the details of Gresley's famous design. No 2582 was built in December 1924 as the last of a batch of 20 'production Pacifics' (2563–82) constructed by the North British Locomotive Co in Glasgow. It was rebuilt as an A3 in December 1941, and as BR No 60083 was withdrawn in May 1964.

NE204, CCB Herbert collection, NRM

Rear

An atmospheric view of the locomotive yard at King's Cross in 1939, captured from the window of a departing train. The famous tunnel is visible just ahead and no doubt HM Lane withdrew his head and closed the window before reaching it! In view is A1 4-6-2 No 2550 *Blink Bonny*, ready to return to its home shed of Grantham, and two unidentified GNR C1 Atlantics. King's Cross was an early convert to colour light signalling.

NE 203, HM Lane

Title page

Thompson B1 4-6-0 No 1268 pauses with its train at Wakefield Westgate in 1948. Although this is a few months into the British Railways era, the scene is pure LNER. Introduced in late 1942, only ten of the B1s were built before the end of the War and the class did not enter full scale production until late 1946. No 1268 was constructed by the North British Locomotive Co in December 1947, a month before the LNER ceased to exist. It was withdrawn in 1964. Just visible behind the engine is an ex-GNR Howlden brake-ended bogie of the late 1890s.

NE162, HM Lane

Introduction

Pre-1955 railway slides in colour of any kind are scarce and pre-1948 views are rare. In 1994 Atlantic Transport Publishers brought out a landmark book called *The Big Four in Colour* by David Jenkinson (with John Edgington and John Smart) which brought together a collection of over 300 colour images taken on our railways between 1935 and 1950. This book was based largely on the collection of images amassed by Ron White of ColourRail over many years. At that time *The Big Four in Colour* contained virtually every available colour image from this period that had been discovered.

In the years since 1994, ColourRail has unearthed additional material, particularly on the LNER and, for the first time, it is now possible for Colourpoint Books, in conjunction with ColourRail, to produce a colour album devoted exclusively to the LNER. *LNER Locomotives in Colour 1936–48* contains 81 images of LNER engines and trains, all in LNER livery and all but one taken in the period 1936–48. None of them were previously published in *The Big Four in Colour*, which itself featured 70 LNER images. The majority of images date from the late 1930s and in the case of the HM Lane archive the dates quoted in captions are 'guesstimates'. Naturally, in a book of this nature, balance is difficult to achieve. We are very much limited by what the photographers chose to capture on film and the geographical areas in which they operated. This book has a strong bias towards the former North Eastern section of the LNER and particularly towards York. Nevertheless, the pictures have captured a wide variety of locomotive types, including a lot of goods engines and some real rarities like the B13 counter-pressure locomotive, an A3 Pacific with feed water heater still fitted and one of Gresley's two P1 2-8-2s. A total of 44 locomotive classes are illustrated on these pages, not to mention a further five sub-classes.

By far the most significant new archive to be unearthed since 1994 is the HM Lane collection. Although some new material by other photographers has appeared, especially for the immediate post-war years, it is dwarfed by that of Lane, fifty of whose images make up the core of this book. A few have not been included, mainly pictures repeating classes already covered in the book or similar views to those chosen. With one exception, I have also deliberately passed over material depicting the early years of BR.

Hubert Meredith Lane lived at Wakefield in the West Riding of Yorkshire. He was born in 1876, the eldest son of a former vicar of Normanton, the Rev W M Lane. His early work was in Hull and Staleybridge, but most of his working life was spent at the British Jeffrey Diamond Company, where

HM Lane

he became the Sales Manager before he retired. He died in January 1959 at the age of 82 and we are indebted to his granddaughter for making his unique photo archive available.

Hubert Lane photographed in monochrome as well as colour and was a pioneer in stereoscopic transparencies. Most of his Dufay images in this book came from stereoscopic slides. The shape of the mounts obliged Lane to crop his slides on each side to fit the mounts and this, rather than any defects in his ability as a photographer, accounts for images with missing buffers at front or rear!

As well as photography, he was a keen railway modeller. He built a 2½" gauge garden railway in conjunction with his friend Mr Harrison. After his marriage in 1913 (to Mr Harrison's sister) he produced what was reputed to be the largest indoor gauge one model railway ever made, 316 feet in length, requiring five helpers to operate and circling the whole house three times at different levels. He was a keen member of the West Riding Small Locomotive Society.

Two main types of colour film were available to early colour photographers. These were Dufaycolor and early Kodachrome, which worked at 2 ASA and 8 ASA respectively. Given that modern emulsions work at 100 or 200 ASA, it is amazing that they captured any images at all. It is not generally realised the late 1930s colour film was of better quality than that available between 1946 and 1950, which suffered from inferior materials due to shortages.

Finally, could I say that this book would not have appeared without the major input of Ron White of ColourRail who has been an enthusiastic supporter of Colourpoint ever since he saw our first colour production in 1994. "Young man, you are doing a cracking job..." etc, etc. Ron has pressed me for years to publish the HM Lane archive. Well Ron, here it is!

Norman Johnston

Our first view dates from June 1936 and was taken at Romford in Essex, where B17 4-6-0 No 2858 has just been named *The Essex Regiment*. No 2858 had been built a month earlier and for a few weeks was named *Newcastle United*. The 25-strong B17/4 batch (2848–72) were built for the Great Central section and had 4200 gallon tenders. They were known popularly as the 'Footballers'. Also on display are two former GER engines – Nos 8579 (B12 4-6-0) and D16/3 4-4-0 No

8900 *Claud Hamilton*. Aside from the locomotives, this scene is full of mid-thirties atmosphere – boys in school caps, ladies in hats and coats, and everyone taking the opportunity to swarm all over the engines – middle class England at play, 1936 style! The men in military uniform are officers and men of the Essex Regiment who had taken part in the naming ceremony for No 2858.

NE117, The Pendragon Collection

The 'Queen of Scots' prepares to depart from Leeds in 1936, headed by A1 Pacific No 2555 *Centenary*, fitted with a non-corridor tender. The first twelve A1 4-6-2s were Nos 4470–81 built at Doncaster in 1922–23. These were followed by 40 'production Pacifics' built in 1924–25 and split between Doncaster (2543– 62) and the North British Locomotive Co (2563–82). No 2555 was built in 1925 and rebuilt to Class A3 in 1944. However, in this view it has been fitted with long-travel valves (1927) as evidenced by the flat box on the running plate above the cylinders. To the right is Ex-GNR N1 class 0-6-2T No 4594, one of four (in this class of 55) built in 1912 for service in the West Riding.

NE151, HM Lane

A delightful view at Hitchen yard in 1937. Contrasting the LNER green and black liveries we have two ex-GNR locomotives. Nearest is Ivatt D2 4-4-0 No 4337 built in 1899, one of a class of 70. No 4337 had been superheated in 1935 and was withdrawn in 1948 as No 2163 (its identity under the 1946 renumbering). Alongside the D2 is C1 class 4-4-2 No 3272. This engine, built in 1904, was the first series production Ivatt Atlantic, following the prototype No 251 (LNER 2251) of 1902. In the background is the coal tipper and on the left the vitally necessary water-softening plant. (Those solid chalk cutting walls, visible in the background, demanded it.) Note the LMS coal wagon behind No 4337.

NE16 ColourRail

The atmosphere of King's Cross in 1937 is well captured in this view of A1 Pacific No 2550 *Blink Bonny* about to depart with a train for Leeds and Harrogate. In the distance a C1 4-4-2 on pilot duty blows off near the Gasworks Tunnel, whilst a second of this type is in the locomotive yard. Two platform staff chat to the driver and the scene includes a nice Gresley side corridor brake/third.

NE150, HM Lane

Our first scene featuring GCR locomotives allows us to contrast two related classes of Robinson 4-6-0s. On this page we have 'Lord Faringdon' class (LNER B3) No 6165 *Valour* on shed at Neasden in August 1937. There were only six members of this class and we are fortunate to have this colour shot of *Valour*, which was the GCR war memorial engine. She was built in 1920 and withdrawn in 1947. The B3 class had 6'9" driving wheels and four 16"x 26" cylinders. Another B3 shot appears on page 52.

NE42, L Hanson

At the same location and date is visually similar B7 class 4-6-0 No 5474. These engines were almost identical but had 5'7" wheels for mixed traffic duties. Twenty-eight of the class were built in 1921–22 and a further ten (5475–85) by the LNER in 1923–24. This engine was one of the GCR examples and was built at Gorton in 1922. All lasted to BR days but only eleven survived long enough to get BR numbers. No 5474 became 61707 and was scrapped in June 1949. Apart from livery and smaller splashers on the B7, there is little to distinguish the two types.

NE43, L Hanson

HM Lane photographed many former NER locomotives in colour and chose his subjects very carefully. One of his rarest shots is this view of B13 (NER S class) 4-6-0 No 761 in 1937. Forty engines of this class were built by Wilson Worsdell at Gateshead in 1899–1909. By 1934 all but ten had been withdrawn and by 1938 only No 761 was left. No 761 survived because it became the LNER counter-pressure testing locomotive in 1934. For this function it was steamed in backward gear to provide a load for locomotives on test. It is seen here with the LNER dynamometer car at York shed, with some testing apparatus still fitted to the left hand cylinder, the gland of which has given up the unequal struggle. This engine became 1699 in 1946 and survived until 1951.

NE163, HM Lane

Another fairly rare type to be recorded in colour was the B15 4-6-0 (NER S2 class), all of which had gone by 1947. No 813 is seen in steam at York shed in 1937. There were 20 members of the class, built by Sir Vincent Raven in 1911–13 with 6'1¼" drivers and 20"x 26" cylinders. Withdrawal began in 1937 when five were scrapped. The others were taken out of traffic in 1944–47. No 813 was built in 1912 and withdrawn in 1944.

NE164, HM Lane

Numerically the largest class of NER 4-6-0 was the 70 strong B16 class (NER S3). These were mixed traffic machines with 5'8" driving wheels and three 18½"x 26" cylinders, all driving the leading coupled axle. Thirty-eight were built by Raven in 1919–22 and a further 32 by the LNER in 1923–24. All survived to 1959 and beyond. In this 1937 view, at its home shed of York, No 847, constructed in early 1920, is still largely in 'as built' condition. However in 1945 it was rebuilt by Thompson with three sets of Walschaerts gear to Class B16/3. In this form it resembled No 2364 opposite, though with left hand drive.

NE209, HM Lane

The B16 class had three sets of Stephenson gear, the eccentrics for which were all on the leading coupled axle, along with the cranks for the inside cylinder! In 1937–40 Sir Nigel Gresley rebuilt six of them with two outside sets of Walschaerts valve gear and one set of conjugated gear for the inside cylinder, producing Class B16/2. This would have made for a much stronger crank axle. At the same time he raised the running plate and fitted new cabs so that the rebuilds took on the appearance of small wheeled 'Footballers' (see page 15). No 2364, rebuilt in June 1937 was the first of the B16/2s and is seen at York shed, probably in 1938. It survived as BR No 61435 until 1964.

NE166, HM Lane

Although the A4 Pacifics were the main headline grabbers for the LNER in the mid 1930s, the new V2 class 2-6-2s featured heavily in LNER publicity as well. The status of these engines is emphasised in this 1937 view showing the class leader, No 4771 *Green Arrow*, on display at an open day at New Barnet. These events were very popular with the general public and not just enthusiasts. The crowd encompasses all ages and all styles of head gear. The first five engines of this class (4771–75) were built at Doncaster in 1936. This three cylinder design has many features in common with the Gresley Pacifics and often deputised for them on express duties. Note the numbering of the exhibits and the rail mounted cranes in the background, which would lift visitors in open wagon bodies, swing them through 360°, and deposit them shaken, if not stirred, on terra firma. The charge of ½d (later rising to 1d) went to railway charities, not the H&SE!

ColourRail NE28

Also on display at New Barnet on this occasion was B17/4 4-6-0 No 2848 *Arsenal*. As mentioned earlier, this 25-strong batch of B17s were named after famous football clubs. No 2848, completed in March 1936, was the first of them. Nos 2848–61 were built in 1936 and 2862–72 in 1937. Withdrawal took place in the late 1950s, this particular engine going in December 1958. The human interest in this scene is immense, with a preponderance of women and children. In the left foreground there appears to be a weighing machine to add to the entertainment but what is that chap sitting on the running plate of 2848 doing? There seems to be something interesting in his suitcase.

NE116, The Pendragon Collection

This A7 class of the North Eastern Railway were the first standard gauge 4-6-2T locomotives in this country, the wheel arrangement having been first used by the narrow gauge Londonderry and Lough Swilly Railway in 1899. Twenty of these 87½ ton locomotives were built at Darlington in 1910–11 utilising scattered numbers between 1113 and 1195. They were intended for heavy coal traffic between the coal mines and the Tyneside docks. Their 4'7¼" wheels and three 16½"x 26" cylinders gave them a tractive effort of 26,140 lbs. No 1174, seen here at Dringhouses yard in 1937, had been superheated in 1930 and had lost its original Ramsbottom safety valves in favour of the Ross pop type. The entire class became LNER Nos 9770–89 in the 1946 renumbering, No 1174 ending its days as BR No 69776 in 1954.

NE160, HM Lane

Weighing in at a comparatively modest 54 tons 4 cwt, the ex-NER G5 0-4-4Ts were in a different league from the mighty A7s. Nevertheless, No1786 makes an attractive colour picture at Neville Hill shed in 1937 as the sunlight catches its black livery with red lining. After June 1928 the red lining ceased to be applied to goods engines and small tank engines. A total of 110 of these suburban tanks were built at Darlington by Wilson Worsdell between 1894 and 1901. They had 5'1¼" wheels and 18"x24" cylinders. No 1786, built in 1896, retains its Ramsbottom valves but the pump for the Westinghouse brake (originally in the cab) has been moved to the front of the left-hand side tank. All 110 survived into BR days and the last went in 1958. No 1786 was withdrawn as BR No 67274 in December 1958.

NE186, HM Lane

Closely related to the 'M' class was the 'Q' class, or LNER D17/2 class. These had a half inch more in cylinder diameter. Thirty were built at Gateshead by Worsdell between 1896 and 1897 (Nos 1871–80, 1901–10 and 1921–30). Once again withdrawals were heavy in the 1930s, with all but seven gone by 1939 and another five before the end of the War, leaving only 1873 and 1902 to soldier on until 1948. Although not of great quality this, like the photo above, is the only known colour picture of the class and shows a grimy No 1873 stopped at Harrogate with the blower on and steam escaping from the valves.

NE176, HM Lane

Seven classes of NER 4-4-0 were inherited by the LNER (D17–D23). Four types had already gone by 1935 leaving Classes D17, D20 and D21 to be represented in this colour book. The oldest of these were the D17/1s (NER Class M), built by Wilson Worsdell at Gateshead in 1892–94. No1629 of this class is seen taking water at York shed in 1937.

There were originally twenty D17/1s (1620–39) but when this photo was taken only Nos 1621, 1624, 1629 and 1636 remained in traffic. These small engines had 7'1¼" driving wheels and 19"x26" cylinders. The last two (1621 and 1629) were withdrawn in 1945.

NE175, HM Lane

The much more numerous D20 class 4-4-0s have fared rather better in the colour archives with at least five images surviving. A total of 60 of this type were built between 1899 and 1907 and all were superheated between 1912 and 1929. No 1207, seen here at Clifton carriage sidings, was one of the last to be built. Originally NER Class 'R', they had 6'10" diameter wheels and generous 20"x26" cylinders. Their 4'9" diameter boilers made them impressive machines. No 1207 retains the original frames but, on rebuilding, twelve engines were given extra deep frames (as seen on No 2020 on page 39) with a convex, rather than a concave, curve at the front.

NE178, HM Lane

With the slow emulsion speed available on the Kodachrome and Dufay films of the 1930s (typically 2 ASA!) it was virtually impossible to capture a moving train, even in sunny conditions. However, KH Leech has pulled it off with this striking shot of a Great Northern Class C1 Atlantic in full flight at Brookmans Park, with a down local made up of Gresley 'Quad Arts'. Perhaps the engine was moving more slowly than it appears! The Ivatt large-boilered Atlantics were introduced in 1902 and carried a 5'6" diameter boiler with a wide 'Wootten type' firebox. No 4451 was constructed in 1908, the last of the main series which comprised 80 engines built in 1904–08.

NE62, KH Leech

In 1910 a further ten Atlantics were constructed at Doncaster (Nos 4452–61) to an improved design, incorporating a modified boiler with 24 element superheaters and eight inch piston valves. Superheating was later extended to the earlier engines. This broadside view shows No 4460, one of the 1910 batch, at King's Cross shed as running in 1937. This angle emphasises the closeness of the front driving wheels to the bogie. Just visible beyond No 4460 is No 359, a J6 0-6-0.

NE63, KH Leech

In the 1930s the NER Atlantics were still very much in evidence, though the Gresley Pacifics had ousted them from the duties they had dominated up to 1923. A total of 72 Atlantics were built for the North Eastern, made up of 20 V & V/09 class (LNER C6), 70 Z class (LNER C7) and the two Smith compound Atlantics (LNER C8). The C8s had already gone by 1935 but we are fortunate to have colour slides showing the others. Class C6 4-4-2 No1680 was the fifth of the first batch of ten Worsdell V class two-cylinder Atlantics, built in 1903–04. This view shows the steam reverser cylinder fitted to this engine. The C6s were withdrawn in 1943–48.

NE170, HM Lane

The C7 class 4-4-2s (NER Class Z) were designed by Sir Vincent Raven who became CME of the NER in 1910, just as the second batch of C6s was emerging from Darlington. The Raven Atlantics were three cylinder machines and weighed over 79 tons. No 717 was one of the first batch of ten, built in 1911 with saturated boilers. In this 1937 view it is leading C7/2 4-4-2 No 732 from the coaling plant at York shed. The second batch of ten (of which No 732 was one) were also constructed in 1911, but were superheated from new. All 20 were built by the North British Locomotive Company. The tender seen here on No 717 was one of the self-trimming ones built for Nos 2193–2212 (see next page), which were easily identified by their very short coal rails.

NE171, HM Lane

After the initial 20 C7s, 30 more followed, in three batches – Nos 2163–72 in 1914, Nos 2193–2204 in 1914–15 and, finally, Nos 2205–12 in 1916–17. All were built at Darlington and were superheated from new. No 2169 was from the first of these batches and, in this view, shows a distinctly lighter green livery than No 717 in the previous shot. This difference may be partly to do with the vagaries of 1930s film emulsions. Unlike most LNER 4-4-0s, the Atlantics retained the dignity of green livery throughout the 1930s. Like many of HM Lane's pictures, the picture was taken at York shed and the low sun allows us to enjoy the richness of the lining out on the frames and splashers. The entire C7 class was withdrawn between 1942 and 1948, only 14 surviving into the first few months of the BR era.

NE173, HM Lane

One interesting feature of the HM Lane colour archive is that he chose the subjects of his photographs very carefully and rarely photographed two engines of the same type unless there were significant differences between them. Thus several slides depict rather unique engines. This is a case in point. In December 1933 No 732 was rebuilt with Lentz rotary-cam poppet valve gear, a new cab and a higher running plate. No 2212 was similarly rebuilt in 1936 but she had originally been built with Uniflow cylinders. Seen here at York shed, the cosmetic changes make No 732 resemble an elongated 'Hunt' 4-4-0 (Page 41).

NE172, HM Lane

Another famous Atlantic design was the Great Central C4 class 4-4-2. Here we see No 5194 at York shed in 1937. The Robinson Atlantics were nicknamed 'Jersey Lilies', after the shapely Edwardian actress Lillie Langtry, who was born in Jersey and was the reputed mistress of the Prince of Wales (later King Edward VII). The alternative explanation of a volupious barmaid (some say prostitute) in the Gorton Works area remains unproven.

No 5194, built in by Beyer Peacock in 1903, was one the original two GCR Atlantics, the other being No 5192. Five more (5263–67) of the type were built by Beyer Peacock in 1904, quickly followed by twelve (6083–94) from the North British Locomotive Co in 1905, and the final eight (5260–62, 5358, 5360–63) built at Gorton in 1906. The 'Heath Robinson' oil pipes add little to her dignity.

NE168, HM Lane

An atmospheric study of A1 4-6-2 No 2548 *Galtee More* about to leave King's Cross in 1937. The photographer has used a slow shutter speed to capture the image within the dark confines of the station roof. *Galtee More* was built at Doncaster in September 1924. It was fitted with long travel valves in 1928 to the condition seen here. As built the A1s had not been noted for their fast running and several experiments with the valves were made in 1925–27 before the ideal setting was decided, combining long lap with long travel. In 1945 No 2548 was rebuilt to Class A3. It became No 517 in the short-lived 1943 renumbering scheme, then No 49 in the 1946 scheme and was finally BR No 60049. It was withdrawn in 1962.

NE149, HM Lane

A major rarity in the ColourRail collection is this slide of Gresley P1 2-8-2 No 2393 on display New Barnet in 1937. Only two of these massive freight engines were ever built and they were specifically designed for hauling long coal trains of up to 100 wagons between Peterborough and London. The two engines, Nos 2393/94 had the same boiler, cylinders and motion as the A1 Pacifics but had 5'2" wheels and a tractive effort of 38,500 lbs, increased to 47,000 lbs when the booster driven trailing truck kicked in. They were built at Doncaster in 1925, but by the time this picture was taken the booster had been removed. With the exception of the LNER 2-8-8-2T Beyer Garrett, which was a banking engine, these were the most powerful freight engines to operate in Britain until the introduction of the BR 9F 2-10-0s in 1954.

ColourRail NE25

A view at Wakefield Westgate in 1937 showing a nice rake of Gresley side-corridor stock. The locomotive at the head of this up train is K3 2-6-0 No 1166. The Gresley K3 Moguls were first introduced in 1920 on the old Great Northern Railway, but only ten (Nos 1000–09) were built before the grouping. However, they soon became an LNER group standard type and a further 183 were built between 1924 and 1937.

They had 5'8" driving wheels and three 18½"x26" cylinders and were very useful mixed traffic engines, equally happy an fast fitted freight and passenger excursion work. The engines carried scattered numbers mainly filling in gaps in the NER sequence. No 1166, seen here, was built by Armstrong Whitworth in 1931.

NE214, HM Lane

In 1923 the LNER inherited no fewer than 2,527 0-6-0 tender locomotives divided into 37 classes (J1–J37). Despite this large number, in early LNER days it was decided that still more 0-6-0s should be built to replace older engines of this type on secondary goods traffic. The result was the J39 0-6-0, 289 of which were built between 1926 and 1938. (There was also Class J38, consisting of 35 similar engines with smaller wheels, built in 1926 for service in Scotland.) The design of the J39 class was based on the NER J27 design (see page 43). The new design had 5'2" driving wheels, 20"x26" cylinders with eight inch piston valves and 5'6" diameter boilers. No 1469 of the class is seen by the water tank at Neville Hill shed in 1937. This engine was built at Darlington in 1932 and scrapped in 1962 as No 64843.

NE189, HM Lane

The largest of the NER 4-4-0s were the D21 class (NER Class R1) which weighed 59 tons without tender. Ten of these (1237–46) were built at Darlington in 1908–09 and superheated in 1912–15. They were a development of the D20 type (page 19) using ten inch piston valves from new and a shortened version of the 5'6" diameter boiler used on the NER Atlantics. The frames were 2'1" longer at the rear to accommodate a 9'0" firebox and there were separate driving wheel splashers. Despite their impressive appearance they were disappointing performers. They also had a prodigious appetite for coal and were unpopular with firemen. Nevertheless, in this 1937 picture, the crew of No 1242 look proud of their charge as it sits outside Starbeck shed.

NE182, HM Lane

A contrast to the ex-NER machine opposite is provided by this ex-GER 'Claud Hamilton' or D16/3 4-4-0, seen at Peterborough East shed in June 1937. It was built 1906, one of a batch of 70 'Claud Hamiltons' (8790–8859) built in 1904–11 with Belpaire fireboxes. It eventually became BR No 62551 and was withdrawn from Peterborough Spital shed in 1956. No 8840 had been rebuilt as a D16/3 'Super Claud' with a large round-topped boiler in March 1935. The GER built 111 Claud Hamiltons in 1900–1911, with a further ten 'Super Clauds' by the LNER in 1923. Behind No 8840 is 8140, a J19 0-6-0.

NE66, JP Mullett

In what is sadly the only available scene from Scotland in this album, we have a colour slide taken at Fort William shed in September 1937. No 9153 *Glen Fruin* is a D34 4-4-0 (NBR 'Glen' class). Thirty two of these engines were built at Cowlairs in 1913–20. They had 6'6" driving wheels and 20"x 26" cylinders. No 9153 was built in June 1917.

It later became LNER No 2480 and as BR No 62480 was withdrawn in 1959. Note the NBR style 'Glasgow' headboard sitting on the running plate. Behind No 9153 is a K2 2-6-0.

NE48, W Potter

Given the grimy state of this J21 0-6-0 and its surroundings, it is perhaps surprising that No 976 was made the subject of a colour slide, but we should be grateful, as this is probably the only colour record of a J21 in LNER days. No 976 is seen by the coal stage at Neville Hill shed, Leeds, in 1937. The NER was a very heavy user of the 0-6-0 type and bequeathed nine classes to the LNER (J21–J27 and two unclassified types which were fairly soon withdrawn). The J21s totalled 201 and were built by Thomas Worsdell between 1886 and 1894, the last ones emerging under his brother Wilson. No 976 was built in 1889 and withdrawn in 1945.

NE187, HM Lane

Tank engines, particularly humble shunting tanks, tend to be under-represented in colour archives of pre-war steam. This is one of the ex-NER N8 0-6-2Ts, a class which comprised 62 locomotives built by Thomas Worsdell between 1886 and 1890. The first eleven were conventional engines but the remainder were built as Worsdell Von Borries two cylinder compounds. No 345, seen sitting outside Neville Hill shed, was one of these and was built in 1889. All were rebuilt as 'simples' by Wilson Worsdell in 1904–12. No 345 was superheated in 1919 and as BR No 69390 was withdrawn in 1956.

NE194, HM Lane

At the heavy-weight end of NER freight power were the Raven Q6 0-8-0s, built in 1913–21. The class had 120 members and were used on iron ore and coal trains. These powerful engines had 4'7½" wheels and 20"x26" cylinders, giving a tractive effort of 28,800 lbs. They were just about the last class of pre-grouping locomotives to remain in traffic up to the end of BR steam on the NE Region in 1967. No 2220 is seen at York in 'ex-Works' condition. It was built in 1917 and withdrawn in November 1966 as BR No 63377. Note the lack of lining out on the clean black livery, relieved only by the numerals and the red buffer beam.

NE195, HM Lane

Not surprisingly, the colourful streamlined A4 Pacifics were popular subjects for early colour photographers. The first four (2509–12) came out in 1935 in silver-grey livery, followed by nine (4482–87, 4493–95) in apple green in 1936–37. The only known colour pictures in these liveries were published in *The Big Four in Colour* in 1994. The remaining 22 (4462–69, 4488–92, 4496–4500, 4900–03) were turned out in Garter blue in 1937–38 and the others were repainted into this colour by October 1938.

In 1937, Nos 4495 *Golden Fleece* and 4496 *Golden Shuttle* were dedicated to work the new 'West Riding Limited' between London and Leeds (see page 69) and received the special version of the Garter blue livery with stainless steel letters. Here, in late 1937, No 4496 is seen at Wakefield Westgate with an up express, though the teak coach visible suggests it is not the 'Limited'. In 1945 No 4496 was renamed *Dwight D Eisenhower* after the famous American General. It became No 60008 and is preserved at Green Bay, Wisconsin, USA.

NE157, HM Lane

When this photograph was taken in March 1938, No 4489 *Dominion of Canada* was ten months old but already had some history behind it. When built in May 1937 it was finished in green livery and named *Woodcock*. However, within a few weeks it became one of five allocated for service on the new 'Coronation' streamlined train and was given the Garter blue scheme and a new name. At the same time it was given a five-note Canadian chime whistle. In March 1938 it was fitted with a Canadian locomotive bell, presented by the Canadian Pacific Railway, and in this view has just emerged from Doncaster paint shop immediately after being fitted with the bell.

NE148, Friends of the NRM

This interesting pair of photographs depict C7 4-4-2 No 706 and D49/2 4-4-0 No 258 *The Cattistock* waiting outside Scarborough with stock for returning excursions to Leeds in the summer of 1938. No 706 was built by the North British Locomotive Company in July 1911 and was the first of the 50 Raven three cylinder Atlantics. No 258 was one of Gresley's three cylinder 'Hunt' class and dated from 1934. Aside from the engines, the photograph shows some interesting LNER carriages, the typical assortment found on excursion trains. Most are of NER origin, including a non-corridor third behind 707 and two clerestories.

ColourRail NE14

In this view, the same two engines are seen at Scarborough shed earlier in the day. A closer look at No 706 reveals that it has been fitted with a second hand black splasher, presumably following some mishap or other.

NE123, The Pendragon Collection

We first described the former NER D20 class on page 19. No 2020 of this class was one of the twelve to be given the deep Raven frames on superheating in 1914. In October 1936 it was further rebuilt by Thompson (Gresley's assistant) with new cylinders which had ten inch piston valves above the cylinders instead of 8¾" below them, as before. No 2020 also received long travel valves, left hand drive, vacuum brake only, a rebuilt tender and a new cab, becoming Class D20/2. It is seen here at Harrogate in 1937 and was eventually withdrawn in 1956. Note the raised running plate over the coupled wheels. Three other D20s were rebuilt to D20/2 in 1942 (two) and 1948 (one), but without the cosmetic alterations.

NE181, HM Lane

In early post-grouping days the LNER had fulfilled the demand for additional 4-4-0s by building some GCR 'Directors' for service in Scotland. When the need came for more such engines for secondary duties Gresley designed his D49 three cylinder 4-4-0s, a typical Gresley design with piston valves and Walschaerts conjugated valve gear. The first 36 engines appeared in 1927–29 and, being named after Scottish and English counties, were soon christened 'Shires'. The last two (Nos 336 and 352) were given Lenz-patent rotary cam poppet valve gear and classified D49/2. These were successful and in 1932–35 a further 40 were built with this arrangement. No 247 *The Blankney*, of this group was photographed at York in 1938.

NE185, HM Lane

The D49/2s were named after famous fox hunts, and thus known as 'Hunts'. No 235 *The Bedale* is at York in ex-Works condition. No doubt, if one of today's TOCs introduced such a naming policy, they would be boycotted and the trains stoned from the lineside! Comparison of the views on these two pages reveals differences in the valve gear arrangement on each side. This was because the rotary cam was located on the right hand side. Note the circular housing on No 235's cylinder and the cam rod running between it and the valve linkage below the nameplate. The 'Shires' and 'Hunts' were all withdrawn in the period 1957–61 except for No 365 which went in 1952. No 246 *Morayshire* is preserved.

NE184, HM Lane

HM Lane made a point of photographing most varieties of ex-NER 0-6-0 in colour. Two are compared on these pages, both pictures being at York in 1938. On this page is J24 0-6-0 No 1931, built in 1897 and withdrawn in 1951. The 70 members of this were built between 1894 and 1898 as short haul mineral engines. They has 4'7¼" wheels and 18"x24" cylinders as built and had the same boilers as the G5 0-4-4Ts (page 17). Only 20 were rebuilt with superheaters and piston valves, 14 of these receiving 18½" cylinders. No 1931 remained saturated to the end. Note the feed water pipe half way along the boiler.

NE188, HM Lane

The J24s were NER Class P and were steadily enlarged with the P1s (J25), 1898–1902 (page 78), the P2s (J26), 1904–05, and the P3s, 1906–09, seen here. These large mineral engines became LNER Class J27. They were almost identical to the P2s but had 18½"x 26"cylinders instead of 18". A total of 80 were built by Worsdell and none were ever superheated. In 1921, Sir Vincent Raven brought out a superheated version, of which 35 were built in 1921–23, though most of these reverted to saturated in the late 1940s. No 1046 was one of the earlier version and was built in 1908. Like all NER engines it had a generously proportioned cab.

NE212, HM Lane

A nice view at Darlington, showing A4 4-6-2 No 4498 *Sir Nigel Gresley* on an up express in August 1938. This locomotive is in the later version of the Garter blue livery with painted numerals and decals, rather than stainless steel. *Sir Nigel Gresley* was built in November 1937 and was allocated to King's Cross shed. In later years it became No 60007 and as an active preserved engine continues to delight enthusiasts. Note the boy and girl observing the engine from a respectful distance while their father engages the driver in conversation.

ColourRail NE3

With an impressive display of power, sister A4, No 4499 *Pochard*, blasts its way out of York with a down train against a dramatic sky. *Pochard* would not be a familiar name to post-war enthusiasts who will remember her better as No 60002 *Sir Murrough Wilson*. She was built in April 1938 and given the stainless steel lettering. Given that she was renamed as early as April 1939, we are privileged to have a colour picture of her as *Pochard*. The view includes the compartment side of a four compartment Gresley side corridor brake third.

NE158, HM Lane

The general light shunting tank on the NER was the J71 class 0-6-0T which were designed by Thomas Worsdell and built between 1886 and 1895. They had the usual NER 4'7¼" driving wheels, but very small 16"x22" cylinders and only 140 lbs boiler pressure. Some later received slightly larger cylinders. A total of 120 were built and were withdrawn from as early as 1933, their low tractive effort disadvantaging them. In this view No 495 is acting as Clifton carriage sidings pilot and looks quite attractive in clean lined black livery. It was built at Darlington in 1889 and was one of the longest lived, being withdrawn as BR No 68250 in 1959. Note the nice teak corridor brake.

NE190, HM Lane

Another of the NER N8 0-6-2Ts features in this shot of ex-Works No 210 at York shed in 1938. In contrast to J71 No 495 opposite, this engine is unlined, an increasingly common situation with small LNER tank engines in the 1930s. No 210 was built at Darlington on 1886. It had been superheated in 1930 and, since the pipe of the vacuum ejector was fitted in November 1938 is visible running along the top of the boiler, this picture was probably taken around then. Just visible in the background is Sentinel steam railcar *Norfolk*. Fifty of these were built in 1928–31, all named after famous stage coaches.

NE193, HM Lane

Another very rare bird photographed by HM Lane was A3 4-6-2 No 2580 *Shotover*. It is seen here at Platform 15 (now 10) of York station, which then only accessible from the south end. The fruit dock can be seen in the background. The A3 Pacifics differed from the original design in having 220 lbs boiler pressure (A1 180 lbs), 19"x26" cylinders (20"x26"), and a 43 element superheater. No 2580 was one of the North British built A1 Pacifics of 1924 and was rebuilt as an A3 in February 1928, the third A1 to be converted. In 1929 No 2580, along with No 2576, had been fitted with an ACFI feed water heater, just visible in this view above the front driving wheels. The bulge above the smokebox was the chamber in which the hot steam mixed with the cold water. The apparatus was removed in 1939.

NE156, HM Lane

The clock tower at Wakefield Westgate reads 10.32 as V2 2-6-2 No 4784 pauses with an up express in 1938. This engine was one of a batch of 20 (4776–95) built at Darlington in 1937 after the success of the first five (see page 14) in 1936. Immediately behind the engine we have a good view of a Diagram 37A Gresley side corridor brake second with five compartments, one of a type built in 1936.

NE197, HM Lane

Ex-NER C7 class 4-4-2 No 2163 leaving York with an up express. The leading vehicle on the train is a roof-boarded Harris's Bacon & Sausage van, which will run empty to Calne. No 2163 was the first Raven Atlantic to be built at Darlington, the first 20 having been constructed at Glasgow by the North British Locomotive Co. Also visible at the south end of York are a D11 ('Director') 4-4-0 on the through road and, on the right, J71 0-6-0T No 1085 shunting a couple of vans. Although the photographer is working somewhat into the sun this is an interesting scene.

NE124, The Pendragon Collection

A broadside view of C7/2 4-4-2 No 732 at York in 1938, showing its Lenz rotary cam poppet valve gear to advantage. This former NER engine was one of only two to be fitted with the gear. It became No 2963 in 1946 but was withdrawn later that year, swept away in a tide of new B1 4-6-0s. Another Gresley vehicle can be seen behind the engine. No 24323 is a Diagram 114 brake third built in 1937. It had four compartments seating 24.

ColourRail NE15

In a view at Aylesbury in December 1938 we see B3/2 4-6-0 No 6166 *Earl Haig* leaving an up Manchester express. No 6166 was a sister of No 6165 *Valour* featured on page 8 but, unlike 6165, had been rebuilt with Caprotti valve gear to class B3/2. It is particularly pleasing to have this colour view, as the engine was to be further rebuilt by Thompson in 1943 to class B3/3, after which it resembled a B1 and was nameless. It was the only member of the six strong class to survive to BR days and was withdrawn in 1949 as BR No 61497.

ColourRail NE10

We return to former Great Eastern metals for a delightful, but deceptively rural looking, scene at Bishops Stortford in Hertfordshire in 1938. The J15 0-6-0s were the archetypical 'maids of all work' on the GER. First introduced in 1883, a total of 289 were built up to 1913, of which 272 were still in service at the grouping. This example was built in 1912 and withdrawn in 1962. They had 4'11" wheels and 17½"x 24" cylinders. Note the forward position of the dome, the Ramsbottom valves without cover and the air pump on No 7571. Incidentally, the GSR in Ireland adopted a modified form of the LNER classification system and their J15s were similarly sized 'maids of all work', numbering over 100 examples.

ColourRail NE19

The 6'9" Atlantics were one of JG Robinson's most successful designs for the LNER. Thirty-one were built, of which four were three cylinder compounds. The remainder had two 19"x 26" outside cylinders. No 6083, photographed at Lincoln in July 1938, was one of the North British built examples. This broadside view shows its graceful lines to advantage. By this date the GCR Atlantics were being given black livery, although the NER, NBR and larger GNR examples continued to qualify for express passenger green.

NE65, KH Leech

This view of C6 4-4-2 No 696 at York shed in 1938 makes interesting comparison with the earlier 1937 view of No 1680 on page 22. Whilst the first ten of Worsdell Atlantics (1903–04) had concave shaped frames under the smokebox, the second ten (built in 1910) had the convex shape associated with Raven designs. The aesthetic lines of these 76 ton machines were somewhat spoilt by the way the cylinders intersected the low running plate. The splasher arrangement seen here also differed from the earlier engines and was similar to that used on the two Smith compound Atlantics of 1906. The C6 class was withdrawn between 1943 and 1948.

NE169, HM Lane

Ex-GNR C1 4-4-2 No 4419 is seen at Hitchin coupled to a D2 4-4-0. This particular engine dated from 1907. The large cab visible on this engine dated from 1923 when No 4419 was fitted with a 'booster' to improve traction when starting or moving at slow speed. The 'booster' was a small auxiliary engine fitted under the cab which used steam from the boiler to power the Cartazzi wheels under the firebox. Whilst successful in itself, it put additional strain on the boiler, was expensive to maintain and was later removed. Withdrawal of the C1 class Atlantics commenced as early as 1924 and only 17 entered service with British Railways in 1948.

ColourRail NE13

K3 2-6-0 No 2438 at York shed in 1938, wearing 'A' class passenger headlamps. The angle of this view emphasises the enormous size of the six feet diameter boiler. This engine is fitted with a flush-sided 4200 gallon tender, standard from 1929 for new K3s. In 1920, Nos 1000–09 of this class were the first Gresley three cylinder engines to adopt the Gresley-Holcroft arrangement of conjugated valve gear, though an earlier version had been applied to 2-8-0 No 461. In LNER days these engines were painted lined black, as here. The engine depicted was one of 20 built in 1935 by the North British Locomotive Co. Another 50 were built by outside contractors and the balance built by Doncaster (30) and Darlington (93). All were withdrawn between 1950 and 1962.

NE192, HM Lane

This is a lovely study, in rich sunlight, of one of the 15 three cylinder Q7 0-8-0s at York shed. These powerful machines were the last heavy freight locomotives designed by Sir Vincent Raven for the former North Eastern Railway. They had 4'7¼" wheels, three 18½"x 26" cylinders and an impressive tractive effort of 36,965 lbs. Five (901–05) were built in 1919 and a further ten (624–26, 628–34) by the LNER in 1924. The entire class was withdrawn en bloc at the end of 1962 but No 901 has been preserved as part of the National Collection and, along with a Q6, operates on the North Yorkshire Moors Railway.

NE196, HM Lane

Class A8 4-6-2T No 1530 at Neville Hill shed, Leeds in 1938. These locomotives were built as 4-4-4Ts, a rather unusual wheel arrangement found only on three other railways – the MSWJR (two in 1896), the County Donegal Railways in Ireland (two in 1902) and the Metropolitan Railway (eight in 1920). The NER was by far the biggest user, building twenty (2143–620) in 1913–14 and a further 25 (scattered numbers) in 1920–22. They had 5'9" coupled wheels, three 16½"x 26" cylinders with piston valves and 4'9" diameter superheated boilers. They were intended for short distance passenger work but were prone to slipping and unpopular with drivers. They became LNER Class H1. In 1931–36 they were rebuilt as 4-6-2Ts and in their new form lasted to 1957–60.

NE161, HM Lane

Here we have another view of one of the ten D21 class 4-4-0s, described earlier on page 30. No 1246 was the last built and was photographed at Wakefield Westgate on an up 'stopper' in 1938. It was built in 1909, superheated in 1913 and withdrawn in 1943. The beading on the splashers of these engines prevented the application of the number in its usual cab-side position. Note the Westinghouse pump and the venerable six-wheeled brake, with a rather straight-sided appearance, behind the engine.

NE183, HM Lane

This view shows one of the D20 4-4-0s at York shed in snow, probably in early 1938. The winter sun captures the handsome lines of these efficient machines as the driver and fireman observe the photographer with interest. At the front end of the frames the short extension, added when superheating this class required a longer smokebox, can be seen.

Note the Gresley anti-vacuum valve fitted behind the chimney, No 724 was built at Gateshead in December 1906, superheated in 1915 and withdrawn as BR No 62378 in November 1956.

NE210, HM Lane

A4 Pacific No 4500 *Garganey* waiting to leave King's Cross on a sunny morning in the summer of 1938. Since the engine was built in April of that year, it can have been only a few months old when this picture was taken. The sunlight captures the vivid colour of the gold transfer numerals and letters with red shading on the tender and cabside, as well as the Indian red wheels, a feature of the class. No 4500 was another of the A4s to experience a name change, becoming *Sir Ronald Matthews* in March 1939. It spent most of its life allocated to Gateshead. In the 1946 renumbering it became No 1 in the LNER fleet, and then BR No 60001. It was withdrawn in 1964.

NE159, HM Lane

The chief interest in this 1938 view at Kings Cross is in the clutter visible around the station. Note the basket trolley on the near platform, the water crane, the advertising posters on the far platform and the station clock reading five to ten. On the right is A1 4-6-2 No 2554 *Woolwinder*. This engine was not rebuilt to Class A3 until June 1942 and therefore does not have the tell-tale patch on the rear of the smokebox to accommodate the larger A3 superheater. (Compare with No 2573 on page 66).

NE202, HM Lane

Following the construction of the second batch of V2s in 1937 (page 49) a further nineteen were built at Darlington in 1938 (4796–4814) and 28 more in 1939 (4815–42). V2 2-6-2 No 4826 was one of this latter batch and is seen here brand new at York. The engine is equipped with the proper 4200 gallon flat-sided tender, as is No 4843 opposite.

These two photographs show differences between Darlington and Doncaster practice in applying the LNER lined green livery. Note the Darlington practice of lining out the front of the frames, in contrast to the plain frames of the products of Doncaster.

NE199, HM Lane

Ready for the naming ceremony! V2 2-6-2 No 4843 was the first of a new batch of ten V2s (4843–52) built at Doncaster in 1939–40. It is seen brand new at Doncaster in June 1939 and has been prepared for naming as *King's Own Yorkshire Light Infantry*, suitably bedecked with garlands and regimental colours. Note the black cylinder covers, in contrast to the lined green cylinders on the Darlington built locomotive opposite.

NE201, HM Lane

A3 4-6-2 No 2573 *Harvester* at Neville Hill shed in 1939. This engine was another conversion from A1 to A3 and this view shows the main characteristics of the A3 modification to the Gresley Pacifics. The patch on the smokebox above the handrail was to accommodate the 43 element superheater. The flat box on the running plate above the cylinders housed the spindles for the long travel valves. However, No 2573 still has the original A1 style dome and still has right hand drive.

NE155, HM Lane

An interesting view in 1939, showing C7 class 4-4-2 No 2170 coupled to A4 4-6-2 No 4901 *Capercaillie* at York. The Atlantic dated from 1914, whilst the Pacific was built in June 1938 and was virtually new in this shot. The Pacific could well be in trouble since A4s were rarely piloted and there is far too much steam emerging from the front end. No 4901 was one of the final batch of A4s and was the only one to be the subject of two name changes. In September 1942, as *Charles H Newton*, it joined the ranks of those named after company directors.

However, when Mr Newton was then knighted, the engine became *Sir Charles Newton* in June 1943. In this guise, it became BR No 60005 and was withdrawn in 1964. In contrast, the Atlantic was scrapped in August 1943. The picture includes two of York's very fine signal gantries.

NE174, HM Lane

Bovril and Virol feature heavily in the background of this King's Cross arrival shot in 1939. Does "Train cooks to use Bovril" constitute an announcement about LNER dining cars, or represent an injunction to passengers wealthy enough to employ cooks? No 4466 *Herring Gull* provides another example of the photogenic qualities of the Garter blue livery. This angle highlights the red lining at the edge of the black smokebox. No 4466 was completed in January 1938 but was renamed *Sir Ralph Wedgwood* in January 1944, after the first A4 to bear that name (4469) was destroyed in a German air raid in 1942. No 4466 was one of only four A4s to carry its 1943 scheme number, which made it 605. It later became 60006 and lasted to September 1965.

NE92, CS Perrier collection

A major colour rarity is this view of the up 'West Riding Limited' ready to depart from Leeds in 1939 not long before the outbreak of war. This is our second view of No 4489 *Dominion of Canada*, complete with its Canadian Pacific bell and whistle (see page 37). The inclusion of the 'West Riding Limited' stock in Garter blue and white (officially Marlborough blue) illustrates the visual impact of the livery when applied to both engine and train. Since 4489 is in less than pristine condition in this view, it may have been covering a failure of one of the regular A4s (4495/6) on this train. In later years No 4489 became No 60010 and, since its withdrawal in May 1965, it has been preserved in Canada at the Montreal Railway Historical Museum. A total of six out of 35 A4 Pacifics have been preserved.

NE205, HM Lane

Another rare Dufaycolor shot of a moving train in 1939. Ex-GCR C4 class 4-4-2 No 6086 was captured roaring through Wendover with an up express. Wendover was between Amersham and Aylesbury on that section of the Great Central main line that was jointly owned by the Metropolitan Railway and the GCR. The LNER had taken over this route in 1937. Behind the engine is a nice set of roof-boarded Gresley mainline stock. No 6086 was built by the North British Locomotive Co in 1905 and withdrawn in 1949 as No 2910. The last of this great class went in 1950.

NE122, The Pendragon Collection

There were major restrictions on railway photography during the Second World War and colour film in particular was very scarce. This view is from a tiny archive which contains the only known colour picture of British trains during the War. It is all the more remarkable because all the views were taken in the depths of winter. Ex-GNR O2 class 2-8-0 No 3486 passes Brookmans Park with a down freight in January 1941. The lighting is lovely and one can almost hear the engine pounding through the countryside with a crisp three cylinder bark in the still air. The first O2 was built in 1918 (No 3461), followed by ten (3477–86) in 1921. A further 46 were built by the LNER in 1923–34.

NE136, The Pendragon Collection

The reader might by forgiven for asking what this picture is doing in a book about LNER locomotives as, at first glance, it is instantly recognisable as a Stanier 8F. However, this is a rare colour picture of one of the members of this class built by the War Department and acquired by the LNER. As O6 class 2-8-0 No 7659 it is parked at March ashpits in October 1945, a few weeks after the end of the War. Note the abbreviated lettering 'NE' on the tender. These engines, and others used by the GWR and SR, were later absorbed into the BR 487xx series of numbers, this particular engine becoming 48714.

NE24, HN James

This is an extremely rare colour view of an A3 4-6-2 carrying its 1946 number in LNER days. To date, this is the only example to have surfaced and is included here despite its rather tricky cross-lighting conditions, although ColourRail have done wonders with the original. The photograph was taken in 1946 and shows No 56 *Centenary* at Wakefield Westgate on an up express. This same engine featured in a 1936 view on page 5 with its pre-1946 number, 2555. Built in 1925, No 65 was rebuilt as an A3 in August 1944 and was shedded at Copley Hill when this 1946 picture was taken, As BR No 60065 it was withdrawn in 1963 from Grantham. Note the steam collector fitted to the dome on A3s from 1934.

NE154, HM Lane

A2/3 4-6-2 No 500 *Edward Thompson* at York in 1947. The Thompson Pacifics were not as popular with enthusiasts as the Gresley and Peppercorn varieties, the positioning of the cylinders behind the front bogie making them look particularly ungainly. There were basically three types of A2 Pacific. Nos 507–510 (1944–45) were essentially V2s completed as Pacifics and were Class A2/1. Class A2/2 comprised Nos 501–06 (1943–44) which were the famous Gresley P2 2-8-2s rebuilt as Pacifics. No 500 was built new in May 1946 as Class A2/3 and 14 more (511–24) followed in 1946–47. This view shows the basic proportions of the class to good advantage. Note the double chimney.

NE153, HM Lane

Post-war, under Edward Thompson and AH Peppercorn, the LNER moved away from three cylinder propulsion for all but the largest express engines like the A1s and A2s. New standard classes were developed, including the K1 2-6-0, the B1 4-6-0 and the L1 2-6-4T, all with two outside cylinders. The most successful, and the most numerous, of these standard types was the B1 4-6-0, exemplified by No

1029 *Chamois* seen here brand new at Darlington in June 1947 in full post-war green livery. The first ten of this class had been built in 1942–44 as Nos 8301–10 but became 1000–09 in the 1946 renumbering. No 1029 was withdrawn in 1966.

NE208, CCB Herbert collection, NRM

A few of the ex-NER J71 0-6-0Ts were painted green after World War II to serve as station pilots. No 8286, at Darlington shed in 1947, shows the full glory of LNER lined green livery in ex-Works condition. The engine also retains its original Ramsbottom safety valve brass casing and the crew show obvious pride in their spotlessly clean engine. The history of this class was given earlier on page 46. No 8286 was built in 1892 and pre-war had been No 237. It became No 68286 in January 1950 and was withdrawn in June 1952.

NE213, CCB Herbert collection, NRM

Another of Thompson's B1 4-6-0s, No 1018 *Gnu* was photographed by CCH Herbert on a stopper at York in 1947. This engine had been completed at Darlington in February that year and is therefore virtually brand new. The picture gives a good view of early post-war York and in the background an LMS train of Stanier corridor stock is at the platform. Note the horsebox immediately behind *Gnu*. A total of 410 B1s were built, 275 appearing under the LNER and the remainder built for the nationalised British Railways up to 1952. Construction was shared between Darlington (60), North British Locomotive Co (290), Vulcan Foundry (50) and Gorton (10).

NE207, CCB Herbert collection, NRM

The exigencies of war led to the survival of many older engines well into the 1950s. Representative of these is J25 0-6-0 No 5656 seen here at Coxwold in 1948. Coxwold is on the NER route from Darlington to Scarborough, via Pilmoor. The J25 class lay somewhere between the J24s (page 42) and the J27s (page 43). They were really a larger-boilered version of the J24 class, but many were later rebuilt with 26" cylinders similar to the J27s. Wilson Worsdell built 120 of them in 1898–1902, but 44 had already gone before nationalisation. No 5656 has been renumbered by Thompson using shaded letters. It was finally withdrawn in 1959.

NE131, Ernest Sanderson

Okay, its not a locomotive but it is definitely LNER and a rare find in colour! Tyneside electric car No 24195 is at Newcastle Central in December 1948. Although this is almost a year after nationalisation, the car is still in full LNER livery with the small white LNER cigar shaped totem on the side. The car visible on the far platform has already received 'British Railways' lettering. These steel-bodied articulated-twins were originally built in 1937 and initially used a bright vermillion-red and cream livery with aluminium grey roof. In 1941, it was decided that this was too conspicuous for enemy aircraft raiding Tyneside and the livery shown here, with a grey roof, was introduced. Although Brian Haresnape's book on LNER liveries (Ian Allan 1984) quotes the colour of the upper panels as 'Quaker grey', in this view they appear decidedly cream.

NE97, Andrew Dow collection

Strictly speaking this is not an LNER era photograph, as betrayed by the engine in the background wearing BR livery. However, J69 class 0-6-0T No 8568, seen at Stratford shed in November 1954, is significant for this book because it was destined to be the last engine to remain in LNER livery and was not repainted until April 1956. The J69 class was a Holden GER design, consisting of 118 locomotives.

Twenty were built new at Stratford in 1904 and the remainder rebuilt from earlier engines. They had 4'0" driving wheels and 16½"x22" cylinders. No 8568 was built in 1896, rebuilt to J69 in 1904 and withdrawn in 1958.

NE72, TB Owen